TADPOLE STORY

Angela Royston

Published 2011 by
A&C Black Publishers Ltd.
36 Soho Square, London, W1D 3QY

www.acblack.com

ISBN   HB 978-1-4081-3356-9
        PB 978-1-4081-3357-6

This book is produced using paper that is made from wood grown in managed, sustainable forests. It is natural, renewable and recyclable. The logging and manufacturing processes conform to the environmental regulations of the country of origin.

Produced for A&C Black by Calcium. www.calciumcreative.co.uk

Printed and bound in China by C&C Offset Printing Co.

All the internet addresses given in this book were correct at the time of going to press. The author and publishers regret any inconvenience caused if addresses have changed or sites have ceased to exist, but can accept no responsibility for any such changes.

Acknowledgements

The publishers would like to thank the following for their kind permission to reproduce their photographs:

Cover: Shutterstock
Pages: Corbis: Jean Hall/Cordaiy Photo Library Ltd 7, Naturfoto Honal 10; Dreamstime: Christian Bernfeld 17, Dirk Ercken 3, 20, Ou Fei 9, Gedewe 4, George Hopkins 19, Jubalharshaw19 15, Maxim Petrichuk 21, Szefei 5, Zarozinia 18; Photolibrary: Rosemary Calvert 8, Reinhard Hölzl 6; Shutterstock: Tony Campbell 13, Matt Hart 16, Payless Images 12, Snowlena 14, Wolfgang Staib 1, 11.

Contents

My World 4

Starting Out 6

Out of the Egg 8

No More Gills 10

Lots of Food 12

Look – Two Legs 14

Four Legs 16

A Froglet 18

Living on Land 20

Glossary 22

Further Reading 23

Index 24

My World

I am a **tadpole** and I live in a pond. One day soon I will change from a tiny tadpole into a fully grown frog – then I will hop out on to the land!

See me change

I am changing all the time. Read my story and see what happens to me as I grow from a tiny speck into a frog.

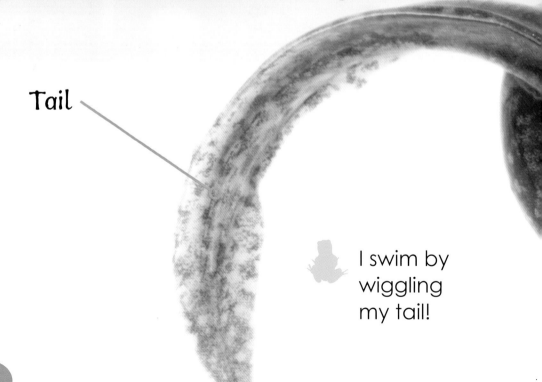

Tail

I swim by wiggling my tail!

Just like mum

One day I shall turn into a frog, just like my mum and dad. Will I look like this?

Starting Out

I began my life as a black dot in a lump of jelly! The jelly is called **frogspawn** and it floated on the surface of the pond.

Bye, Mum!
My mum laid the frogspawn, then she swam away and I never saw her again. Fish eat frogspawn, but luckily they didn't eat me!

Each black dot is a tiny tadpole.

Tadpole

Sticky eggs

Each tadpole grows
inside its own egg.
Sticky jelly holds
the eggs together.

7

Out of the Egg

I grew in the frogspawn for two weeks, then I was ready to **hatch**. I wriggled out of my egg, and clung on to the jelly.

Getting stronger

I ate the jelly and grew stronger and stronger, until I was strong enough to swim away. I had **gills** on the sides of my head.

Not alone

My brothers and sisters hatched out too, so the pond was full of tadpoles.

I used my gills to breathe underwater.

Gill

No More Gills

My gills did not last long.
After just ten days my gills
closed up and I began to grow
lungs inside my body instead.

Up to the surface

Sometimes I swam up to the surface to
eat tiny plants that floated on the water.
I didn't swim to the surface to breathe
in air until my lungs were fully grown.

Eat, eat, eat

Tadpoles love to eat! We swam around the pond looking for tiny plants to eat.

Look – no more gills!

Lots of Food

The more I ate, the bigger I grew. My body became so fat and round that many animals wanted to eat me! It was a dangerous time.

Nearly caught

One day, I was nearly caught by a fish, but I twisted and turned and managed to swim away. Phew!

 My strong tail helped me to swim.

Danger!

The pond is a dangerous place – every animal is lunch for something.

Look – Two Legs

When I was five weeks old, my back legs began to grow. At first they were very small and weak, but they quickly grew bigger and stronger.

Swimming with legs

When I swam, I used my legs as well as my tail, and I grew skin between my toes so I could push against the water.

Leg

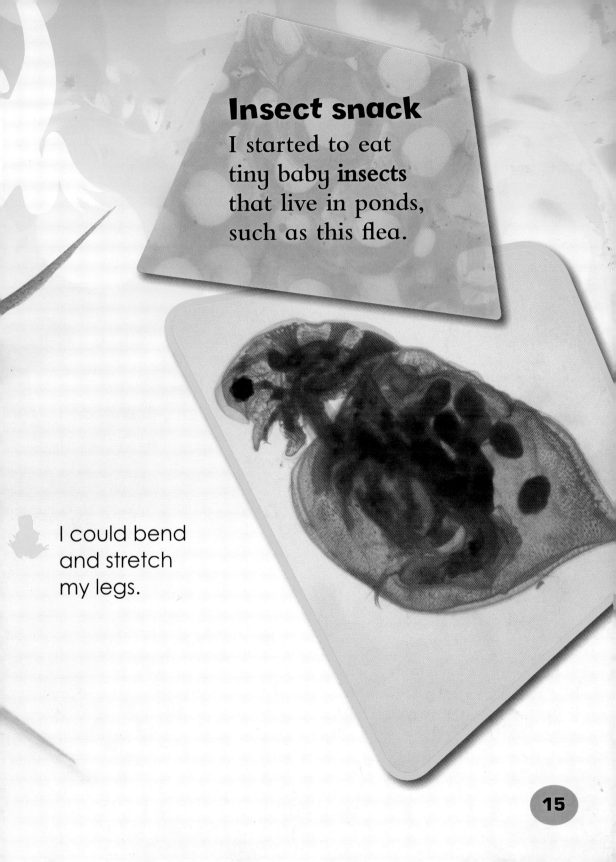

Insect snack

I started to eat
tiny baby **insects**
that live in ponds,
such as this flea.

I could bend
and stretch
my legs.

15

Four Legs

When I was about eight weeks old, two small bumps began to grow on the outside of my body – where my gill slits used to be.

Nearly there

The bumps changed into two legs, so I had four legs altogether, but I still had my tail. I was halfway between a tadpole and a frog – what happened next?

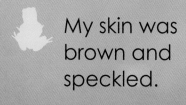

My skin was brown and speckled.

Front Leg

Not me!

This **newt** tadpole lives in the pond. Its front legs grew before its back legs.

A Froglet

By the time I was just 12 weeks old, I had changed into a tiny frog. I had come a long way since I was in the frogspawn.

First jumps

One day I climbed out of the pond and sat on a floating leaf. Then I took my very first jump on dry land!

 Look how short my tail had become!

Teeny weeny

This frog is no bigger than your fingernail! It can sit inside a flower.

Tail

Living on Land

Now I am a year old and I spend most of my time on land, but I never go far from water. I jump in to keep my skin wet.

Hide and seek

It's hard to see me in the water, but I see really well! When a fly comes by, I catch it with my long, sticky tongue.

Eye

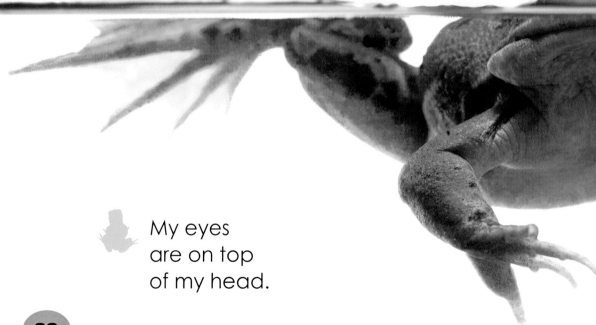

My eyes are on top of my head.

Slithery snake

On land, I watch out for snakes and other animals that might want to eat me.

21

Glossary

frogspawn lots of frog's eggs, stuck together with jelly

gills parts of the body that are used to breathe in water. Tadpoles, fishes, and many other water animals have gills.

hatch when an animal or insect breaks out of its egg

lungs parts of the body used to breathe in air

insects small animals with six legs and often two wings. Flies, butterflies, and ladybirds are all insects.

newt small animal that lives some of its life in water and some of it on land.

tadpole young frog before it has grown legs

Further Reading

Websites

Find out how to tell frogs from toads at:
www.42explore.com/frogs.htm

You can find lots of information about tadpoles and frogs, and fun things to do, at:
www.allaboutfrogs.org

This website has lots of facts about frogs, with activities and worksheets too. You can find it at:
www.enchantedlearning.com/subjects/amphibians/frogs

Books

From Tadpole to Frog by Anita Ganeri, Heinemann Library (2006).

Tadpole to Frog by Camilla de la Bédoyère, QED (2009).

Tadpoles and Frogs (Usborne Beginners) by Anna Milbourne, Usborne (2002).

Index

breathing 9, 10

eating 8, 10–11, 12, 15, 20
eggs 7, 8
eyes 20

fish 6, 12
fly 20
frog 4, 5, 6, 18–19, 20–21
froglet 18–19
frogspawn 6–7, 8

gills 8, 9, 10, 11, 16

hatch 8–9

insects 15

jelly 6, 7, 8
jump 18, 20

legs 14, 16–17
lungs 10

newt 17

plants 10–11

skin 14, 16, 20
snakes 21

tail 4, 12, 14, 16, 18, 19